W9-DBH-312

THE FLU

THE FLU

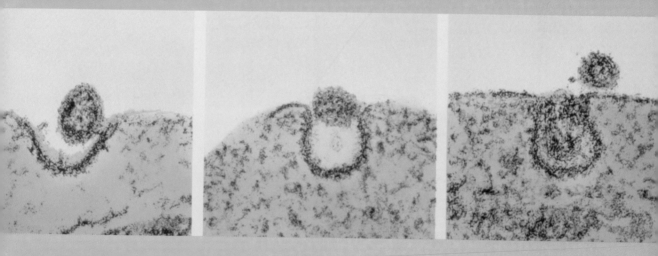

Gretchen Hoffmann

 **Marshall Cavendish**
Benchmark
New York

With thanks to Adam J. Adler, Ph.D, Associate Professor, Center for Immunotherapy of Cancer and Infectious Diseases and Department of Immunology, University of Connecticut Health Center, for his expert review of the manuscript.

Marshall Cavendish Benchmark
99 White Plains road
Tarrytown, New York 10591-9001
www.marshallcavendish.us

This book is not intended for use as a substitute for advice, consultation, or treatment by a licensed medical practitioner. The reader is advised that no action of a medical nature should be taken without consultation with a licensed medical practitioner, including action that may seem to be indicated by the contents of this work, since individual circumstances vary and medical standards, knowledge, and practices change with time. The publisher, author, and medical consultants disclaim all liability and cannot be held responsible for any problems that may arise from the use of this book.

Library of Congress Cataloging-in-Publication Data

Hoffmann, Gretchen.
The flu / by Gretchen Hoffmann.
p. cm. — (Health alert)
Summary: "Explores the history, causes, symptoms, treatments, and future of different types of influenza"—Provided by publisher.
Includes bibliographical references and index.
ISBN-13: 978-0-7614-2208-2
ISBN-10: 0-7614-2208-0
1. Influenza--Juvenile literature. I. Title. II. Series: Health alert (Benchmark Books)

RC150.H56 2007
616.2'03--dc22
2006011980

Front cover: An influenza virus
Title page: The flu virus infecting a cell
Photo research by Candlepants, Incorporated

Front cover: Dr. Linda Stannard, UCT / Photo Researchers Inc.
The photographs in this book are used by permission and through the courtesy of:
Photo Researchers Inc.: Dr. Steve Patterson, 3, 11, David Parker, 5; Stem Jems, 12; James Cavallini, 13, 22; Keith R. Porter, 14; VEM, 15; Science Photo Library, 27; James King-Holmes, 28; Pasieka, 35; Scott Camazine, 41; Michael Donne, 43; George Olson, 49; BSIP, 51; Hattie Young, 53. *Corbis*: Grace / ZEFA, 7; Howard Sochurek, 9; Michael A. Keller / zefa, 17; tsu Yasukawa / Star Ledger, 25; Mediscan, 24; 30; Bettmann, 32, 33; Viviane Moos, 37; Popov Gennady / ITAR-TASS, 45; Dadang Tri / Reuters, 56. *Getty Images*: 3DClinic, 16; Science Faction, 18; Digital Vision, 38; Stone, 54. *Bibliotheque Nationale, Paris, France, Lauros / Giraudon / Bridgeman Art Library*: 26. *Jacques Boissinot / Canadian Press / Phototake USA*: 47.

Printed in China
6 5 4 3 2 1

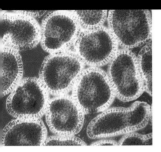

CONTENTS

WHAT IS IT LIKE TO HAVE THE FLU?

Billy and Suzanne were getting excited—only two more weeks to go before winter vacation. Suzanne, a sixth grader, was studying hard for a big math test. In the fourth grade, Billy was busy finishing a science project. One day, two classmates working on the project stayed home sick from school. Then another of Billy's classmates started feeling hot and achy and went to the school nurse. She sent him home.

When he got home, Billy discovered someone else was sick—Suzanne. She could not even get out of bed. "My throat is so sore, I can hardly swallow. And I have a bad headache, too," she told her parents. "It hurts when I move." After a quick call to the family doctor, Suzanne's parents learned that the flu was going around. Many adults and kids were sick from it all over town. The doctor said Suzanne probably had it and should stay home from school for the next week or so.

The flu that made Suzanne so miserable is a common illness that a **virus** causes. The flu virus infects millions of people every year. It can cause high fever, cough, sore throat, runny or stuffy nose, headaches, muscle aches, and extreme tiredness. Chances are good that if one person has the flu, another person he or she lives with, goes to school with, or works with also has it. This is because the flu is highly **contagious** and passes easily from person to person.

The next day, Billy began to feel sick, too. Soon he had all the same flu **symptoms** as his sister. He and Suzanne spent the rest of the week recovering at home. They rested on the couch or in bed, drank plenty of water and juice, and took the pain-relief medication their doctor had recommended to their parents.

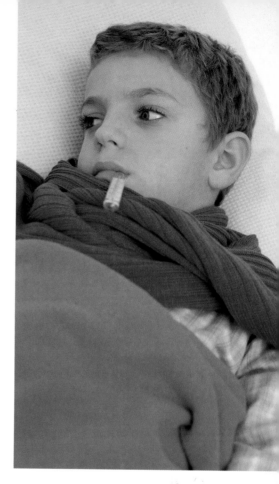

Most people suffering from the flu feel tired, achy, and feverish for about a week.

Luckily, the children's parents did not get sick. They were protected from the flu because they had received flu shots at their jobs. A flu shot is an injection of **vaccine** that helps prevent people from getting the flu.

By the following week, Billy and Suzanne both felt well enough to go back to school. Like most of the people who got the flu around the same time they did, Billy and Suzanne completely recovered after spending a few miserable days sick at home.

WHAT IS THE FLU?

The flu is an infection of the airways, throat, and lungs caused by the influenza virus. Like all viruses, influenza viruses are microscopic **parasites.** That means they are completely dependent on living organisms called **hosts.** Viruses reproduce by infecting hosts such as animals, birds, insects, plants—or you!

The virus infects between 5 and 20 percent of the population in the United States every year. If the flu breaks out in your school or neighborhood, one or two people out of every ten people you know will probably get sick. All of that adds up to about 38 million missed days of school. Adults with the flu miss approximately 70 million days of work. All these missed workdays add up to billions of dollars in lost labor.

People do not just miss school and work because they get the flu. More than 200,000 flu victims need to be hospitalized each year in the United States alone. And each year, approximately 36,000 of them die from the effects of the flu. Around the world, influenza affects about three to five million people

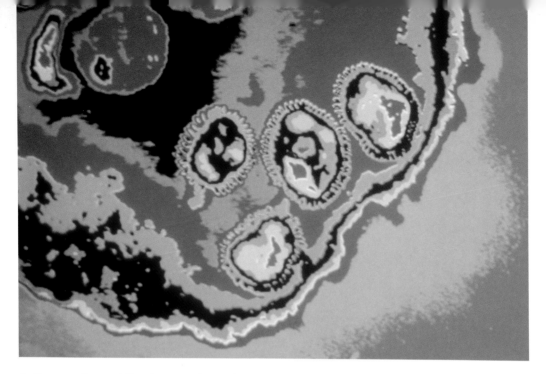

Influenza viruses like the one shown in this magnified image cannot survive on their own for more than several hours.

every year. Between a quarter-million and a half a million of them die from flu complications.

Despite so many flu victims, most people do not get the flu every year. There are several reasons for this. Some people do not come into contact with the flu virus. Others get protection with flu shots. Still others can fight off some flu infections thanks to their hard-working **immune systems,** which defend the body from harmful invaders like flu viruses.

THE IMMUNE SYSTEM

Your immune system is always on the job, observing all types of cells and materials traveling though your body. Certain cells, chemicals called **proteins,** and organs in your immune system identify foreign invaders, like flu viruses, that can make you

The Flu Season

···································

People are more likely to get the flu between October and April. The worst months for infection in the northern hemisphere are December through March. Scientists are not completely sure why this "flu season" exists every year, but they have a few ideas. First, the flu virus survives better in cool and wet weather. It is possible that the viruses can survive longer outside a person's body, as when they are sneezed out, when the weather is cool.

Also, people tend to crowd together during the colder months. Flu viruses have shorter distances to travel because windows are tightly shut. Many holidays also take place during the colder months of the year. Wherever people gather to celebrate, the festivity can become a party for the viruses, too. They can easily move from person to person in a crowded space.

But people can get the flu any time of year, especially due to the number of people who travel around the world. Influenza viruses exist worldwide. People may carry the viruses with them when they travel, exposing fellow travelers regardless of the time of year.

sick. Your immune system can tell the difference between substances that belong in your body and those that do not. When it detects a "nonself," such as a flu virus or other harmful outsider, from a "self," the immune system's defenses kick in. They treat anything unfamiliar as a threat.

These outside threats to our bodies are called **pathogens.** Pathogens, which can also be called **microbes** or germs, may be bacteria or viruses such as influenza. Sometimes the immune system succeeds in keeping out harmful invaders, and sometimes it does not. When your immune system is not able to prevent an

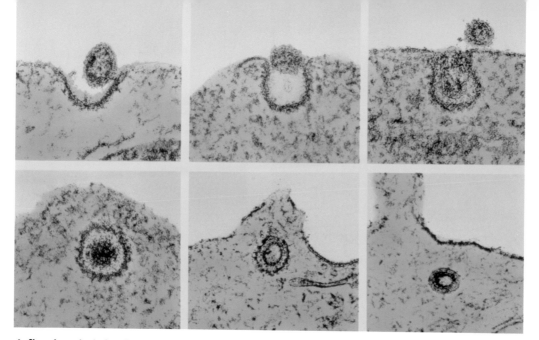

A flu virus is infecting a cell in this electron micrograph. The virus's spiky protein covering attaches itself to the host cell. From there, the virus enters and takes over.

influenza virus from infecting you, you may come down with the flu. However, even when you do get the flu, you begin to feel better when your immune system is able to destroy the virus. And if you received a flu shot, your immune system will respond to a viral infection more quickly so you do not become sick at all, or you are only sick for a short time.

The "first defenders" in your immune system are white blood cells. Just as an army has soldiers with different jobs, your body has different types of white blood cells to defend against invaders. All white blood cells are known as **leukocytes.** These travel swiftly through your body to challenge intruding pathogens. Two kinds of white blood cells, or leukocytes, are called **lymphocytes.** These are either B-cells or T-cells. Each one has a special job.

B-cells produce protective proteins called **antibodies.** These antibodies attach themselves to certain substances on pathogens called **antigens** and mark them so that other cells will destroy them later. Antibodies also block the flu virus from moving from one cell to another. This limits the spread of infection within the body. B-cells can produce up to 10 million copies of the needed antibody in one hour.

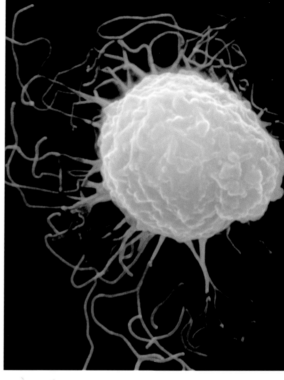

Some kinds of T-cells, like the one in this electron micrograph, can recognize viral or bacterial pathogens that have tried to enter the body in the past.

The job of T-cells is to coordinate the attack on pathogens. T-cells do this by giving instructions to other immune cells on when and how to attack. These immune cells then produce different kinds of **molecules** that carry information and instructions from one group of immune cells to another. These messenger molecules tell other cells when to change their behavior and coordinate the immune response.

Some special B-cells and T-cells also have amazing memories and remember an old infection for a long time. These cells are like soldiers facing an enemy they have fought before. They know the enemy's old tricks and weapons and how to fight them. The T-cells quickly launch an attack, using effective antibodies that worked in the past.

Phagocytes, another kind of white blood cell, work with lymphocytes to destroy germs. But phagocytes play a different role. After leukocytes mark antigens for destruction, phagocytes actually destroy them. They do this by surrounding these harmful invaders, then "eating" them. They digest the invaders and turn them into harmless fragments.

White blood cells work with two important organs in your body: the spleen and the thymus. Your spleen is located in the

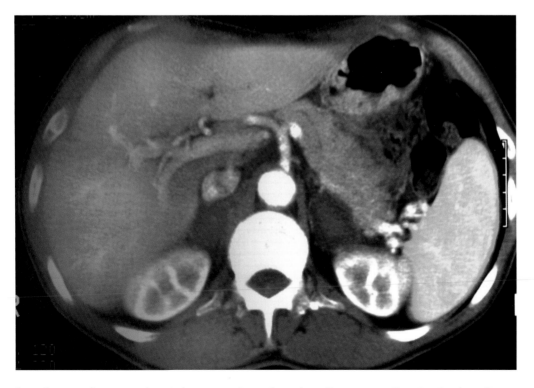

Lymphocytes in your spleen, the organ shown here in yellow, go on the attack when the immune system recognizes a foreign invader trying to enter the body.

upper left side of your abdomen between your ribs and hips. One of the spleen's major jobs is to filter blood. This filtering process removes unwanted material like infection-causing pathogens as well as old or damaged blood cells. The hard-working spleen is also a place where lymphocytes get activated so that they can destroy invading pathogens.

Your thymus is located in the center of your upper chest, and its job is to produce T-cells. T-cells develop in the thymus. There T-cells learn to distinguish between substances that belong in the body and those that do not. T-cells must recognize their immune system teammates to communicate with them. T-cells die when they fail to recognize other immune cells. T-cells also die if they mistakenly target normal body cells for destruction.

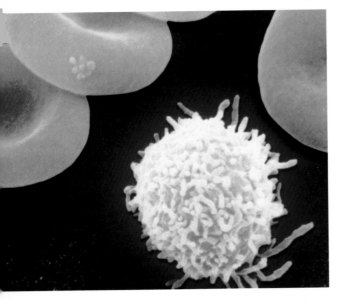

This electron micrograph shows red blood cells and a white blood cell. The white blood cell is a key part of the immune defense against foreign substances such as the flu virus.

Another white blood cell producer in your body is **bone marrow.** This spongy material in your bones plays an important role in the immune system. Blood vessels that run through bone marrow transport blood loaded with white blood cells. Plus, the bone marrow itself produces a variety of blood cells: red blood cells that carry oxygen, platelets that help blood **clot,** and infection-fighting white blood cells. Bone marrow also produces B-cells.

B-cells stay in the bone marrow to complete development. Once they are fully formed, B-cells can produce antibodies against many invaders that try to attack the human body.

The **lymphatic system** works with the immune system to fight attacking pathogens. The entire lymphatic system shares many organs and cell types with the immune system. It consists of lymph vessels, lymph nodes, and lymph fluid. Lymph vessels are similar to veins that carry blood except that they carry a clear fluid instead of blood. This lymph fluid contains waste products from cell activity, proteins, fats, and many white blood cells, especially lymphocytes. These watchful and helpful lymphocytes continually travel through lymph tissue, lymph fluid, and blood.

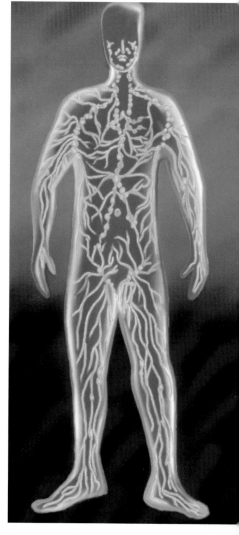

The lymphatic system's network of vessels and tissues filters blood to fight infection.

At certain points in the body, the lymph vessels have checkpoints called **lymph nodes.** These nodes filter lymph fluid and remove foreign material. White blood cells also gather in the

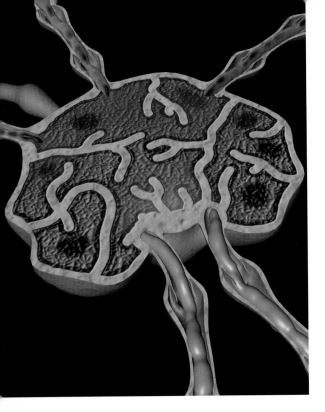

The human body has between 500 and 1,500 lymph nodes like the one shown here.

lymph nodes, the way they do in the spleen. Lymph nodes are good places for white blood cells to monitor and destroy germs floating in the lymph fluid. Everyone has lymph nodes in the sides of the neck, behind the ears, in the back of the head, under the chin and jaw, and in the groin and armpits. When your body is healthy, your lymph nodes are soft and difficult to feel. But when your body is actively fighting an infection, your lymph nodes can become swollen, tender, and more solid. When your infection is over, your lymph nodes return to normal size and feel soft again.

Fighting pathogens is a lifelong battle for your immune system. During your lifetime, your immune system recognizes and remembers millions of pathogens and the antigens associated with them. It can recreate the most effective antibodies if the same pathogen attacks your body again. People exposed to a flu virus similar to one they have already had may be protected from getting that same flu again. This earlier exposure may be one reason why some family members come down with a certain type of flu and other family members do not.

A doctor checks a patient's lymph nodes to see if an infection is present.

VIRAL INFECTION

So, with all these immune system protectors standing guard—white blood cells, organs, bone marrow, the lymph system—why do millions of people still get the flu every year? The answer is that influenza viruses have special features that can overpower a body's immune system. First, influenza viruses are efficient travelers. Second, they have an amazing ability to copy themselves. And, third, they can change so frequently or suddenly that the immune system cannot produce effective antibodies fast enough.

Not only do influenza viruses travel easily from person to person, they do so secretly for part of the time. A person with the flu may be contagious for several days before he or she knows it. This makes it difficult for others to avoid sick people who do not show symptoms yet. When an infected person coughs or sneezes, he or she releases tiny droplets of water from the mouth and nose. These droplets are loaded with the flu virus. The tiny water packages carry the virus through the air and can travel several feet away from the person who sneezed or coughed. If the virus-containing droplet lands on

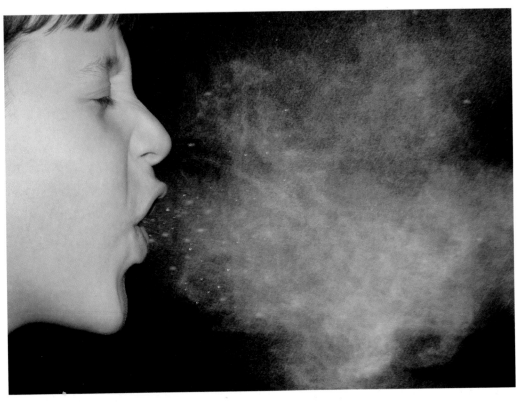

Sneezing is a sign that your immune system is trying to get rid of a foreign irritant that has entered your nose. These irritants may include dust, pollen, or bacteria and viruses. One sneeze, however, can travel and spread a virus as far as three feet away.

someone's mouth or nose, that person may also get sick.

However, a direct hit by a sneeze or cough is only one way to get infected. Flu virus droplets also land on surfaces that many people touch, such as doorknobs or desktops. If another person grabs the doorknob, then touches her lips, scratches her nose, or rubs her eyes, she may pick up the flu virus and also get sick.

The flu virus's ability to turn normal human or animal host cells into flu-copying machines is another reason influenza can take over immune systems. The influenza virus can infect humans and many different animals, including ducks, chickens, pigs, dogs, horses, whales, and seals. While they are outside the hosts' bodies, viruses are able to stay alive for several hours. That means if someone sneezes on a magazine in the morning, then hands it to a friend later on, the friend could pick up the flu virus and get sick.

How Long Is the Flu Virus Contagious?

You start feeling sick from one to four days after you were exposed to the flu virus. Adults generally can spread the virus to others starting one day before they feel sick, and up to seven days after the symptoms start. Children can infect others for much longer. They are **infectious** for several days before they start to feel sick. They can pass the virus on for more than seven days after showing flu symptoms.

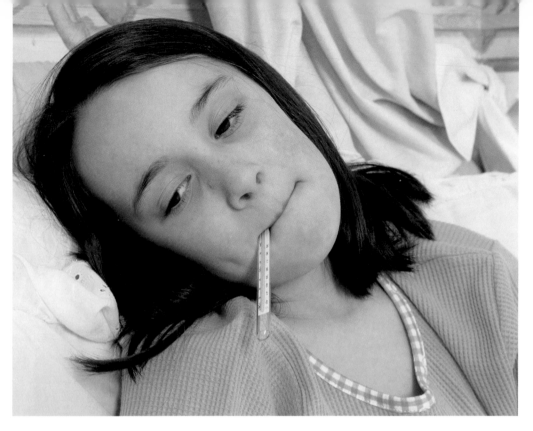

Though a fever is uncomfortable, it is a sign that the body is actively fighting a viral or bacterial infection

Flu Symptoms

Flu symptoms tend to start suddenly. Many people who have had the flu say they went from feeling fine to feeling awful within a matter of hours. And they can almost pinpoint the moment when they started to feel sick.

Almost everyone who has the flu gets a fever. During a fever, your immune system sends special chemicals into your blood. These chemicals signal your brain to heat up your blood to help kill the harmful flu virus. Normal average body temperature for humans is 98.6 degrees Fahrenheit (37 degrees Celsius). Fever is typically highest when flu symptoms first appear. Temperatures can reach 100 °F to 103 °F in adults and even higher in children. Although a fever feels awful, it actually fights for you. Fever activates the immune system to make more white blood cells to attack the invading influenza infection.

Feeling achy is one of the first symptoms of the flu. Muscle pains in your back, arms, and legs—really all over your body—can make it hard for you to even get out of bed. You may also get a cough, a sore throat, and a stuffy or runny nose. Breathing problems are also typical **respiratory** symptoms associated with the flu. Other symptoms usually include chills, sweating, headache, watery eyes, and fatigue or extreme tiredness.

Having the flu drains your energy and makes you feel exhausted. Along with fatigue and a general sick feeling, people with the flu may also lose their appetites. Luckily, most people start to feel better within three to five days. Most people recover completely in one to two weeks.

Other stomach-related problems like nausea, vomiting, and diarrhea can sometimes accompany the flu, but they are not very common or major complaints. Young children are more likely to have these types of symptoms than adults are. Sometimes when someone is throwing up or feeling nauseated, that person may say he has "stomach flu." But an illness of the stomach or intestines should not really be called "flu." Other **microorganisms,** not the influenza virus, cause this illness.

The flu can feel much like other illnesses, such as the

common cold, mononucleosis, and some bacterial infections. While the flu shares many of the same symptoms as the common cold, the flu is generally more severe. For example, the common cold rarely causes a high fever, while the flu is characterized by fever. General aches and pains are also much milder with the common cold than with the flu, as are exhaustion and headache.

Flu Viruses in Action

So what is it about the influenza virus that helps it conquer a host's immune system? Just like the living hosts they infect, flu viruses are made up of **genes.** Genes are a kind of recipe that

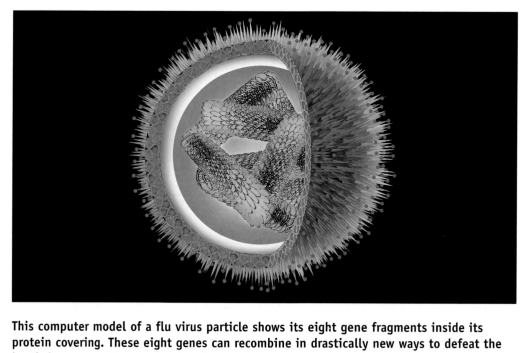

This computer model of a flu virus particle shows its eight gene fragments inside its protein covering. These eight genes can recombine in drastically new ways to defeat the host's immune system.

tells cells how to make all of the proteins an organism needs to survive. Genes are passed on to the next generation when an organism reproduces. But viruses cannot reproduce on their own. Instead they must take over another organism's own cells to reproduce.

Here is how this takeover happens. When the flu virus enters your body, it first attacks cells in your nose or mouth. Then the virus attaches itself to a target cell and makes a hole in its membrane, or covering. Next, the virus inserts its genetic material into the cell's opening. That is when the virus begins to do its damage. It uses the host cell's own natural processes to copy the virus's genetic material and proteins. When the cell is full of the virus's materials, the newly copied viruses burst out. These copies go on to infect neighboring cells, effectively spreading the infection within the same host. Viruses that are sneezed or coughed out of one host can then begin this damaging process in a new host. In this way, the influenza virus spreads its infection from host to host. While all this is happening, the immune system is fighting the virus with a high fever to kill it, and with mucus and watery eyes to shed or excrete the viruses.

Types of Influenza Viruses

If there were only one type of flu virus infecting people, scientists—and immune systems—would have an easier job preventing flu infections. But influenza viruses contain various

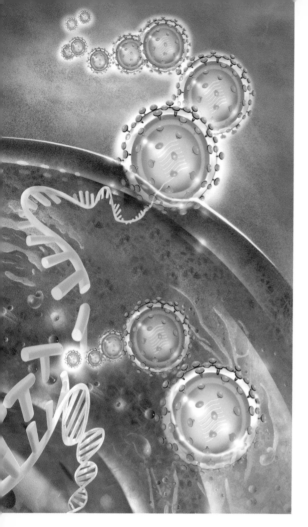

This computer model shows a virus's genetic material (shown in yellow) entering the host in order to make more viruses.

combinations of proteins that scientists call **strains.** These strains are different than the original virus they came from but still have some of the original characteristics.

Currently there are several forms of influenza viruses circulating worldwide. Two of them are different strains of influenza type A. Another is influenza type B. These three are the most common types responsible for the yearly outbreaks. Another influenza, type C, does not cause the widespread infections that A and B do.

Influenza viruses within the A, B, and C strains are constantly changing. This happens when a virus's genetic code changes or **mutates.** Unlike human cells that can "proofread" and fix their own genetic errors, influenza viruses lack that ability. As a result, little errors continually occur and build up until the influenza virus mutates so much, it becomes an entirely new strain.

Antibodies that worked for one kind of flu will not always work against a similar flu with new mutations. When flu virus mutations are tiny and build up slowly, the body's immune

A scientist studies annual flu virus strains in order to develop effective vaccines.

system is able to adapt. It produces slightly different antibodies that match the new virus and defeat it. Antibodies formed during the previous infection may offer partial protection.

This process of gradual change happens repeatedly, with slightly different viruses popping up every year. That is why scientists must develop new flu vaccines every year. However, sometimes changes in influenza viruses happen suddenly. Or the changes involve a large piece of the virus's operating instructions. When dramatic changes occur, people may be unprotected. A virus that undergoes a dramatic mutation looks so different from the original that none of the antibodies waiting to attack can recognize and kill it in time. In this situation, millions of people worldwide can become very sick very quickly. This has happened before, and scientists are trying to learn from history to prevent it from happening again.

3

THE HISTORY OF THE FLU

Scientists do not know for certain how long influenza has been infecting humans. More than 2,000 years ago, the Roman historian Livy described a flu-like disease that attacked the Roman army and the enemy soldiers they were fighting: " . . . both sides were visited by pestilence [disease], a calamity almost heavy enough to turn them from all thoughts of war. . . . In the beginning, people fell ill and died through the effects of the season and the unhealthy locality; later, the nursing of the sick and contact with them spread the disease, so that either those who had caught it died neglected and abandoned, or else

An illustration of the Roman historian Livy who lived between 59 BCE and 17 CE. Over two thousand years later, in 1918, a flu similar to the deadly one that Livy described also killed many young soldiers.

they carried off with them those who were waiting on them and nursing them, and who had thus become infected. Deaths and funerals were a daily spectacle; on all sides, day and night, were heard the wailings for the dead."

As with many illnesses, people did not understand the cause of influenza for many centuries. People in fifteenth-century Italy thought the sickness was caused by the "influence" of the stars, so they named it "influenza." Because influenza viruses are among the tiniest pathogens in existence, researchers could not study them until electron

INFLUENZA

FREQUENTLY COMPLICATED WITH

PNEUMONIA

IS PREVALENT AT THIS TIME THROUGHOUT AMERICA.

THIS THEATRE IS CO-OPERATING WITH THE DEPARTMENT OF HEALTH.

YOU MUST DO THE SAME

IF YOU HAVE A COLD AND ARE COUGHING AND SNEEZING. DO NOT ENTER THIS THEATRE

GO HOME AND GO TO BED UNTIL YOU ARE WELL

Coughing, Sneezing or Spitting Will Not Be Permitted In The Theatre. In case you must cough or Sneeze, do so in your own handkerchief. and if the Coughing or Sneezing Persists Leave The Theatre At Once.

This Theatre has agreed to co-operate with the Department Of Health in disseminating the truth about Influenza. and thus serve a great educational purpose.

HELP US TO KEEP CHICAGO THE HEALTHIEST CITY IN THE WORLD

JOHN DILL ROBERTSON

COMMISSIONER OF HEALTH

Health warnings during the 1918 flu pandemic strongly advised sick people to stay home.

microscopes came into use in the 1930s. The electron microscope made it possible for scientists to observe many viruses, including those that cause the flu.

OUTBREAK, EPIDEMICS, AND PANDEMICS

A flu outbreak occurs when influenza affects many people within a small area, like a town or university, during a short period of time. Such outbreaks of the flu happen every year. When a high percentage of people in a larger geographic area get infected with the flu at almost the same time, this is called an **epidemic.** During an epidemic, the virus spreads rapidly through the population. However, if the same virus infects people in different parts of the world at nearly the same time, this event is called a **pandemic.** A new strain of virus that has never circulated through the population before can cause a

To learn more about the flu, researchers today are analyzing the sample blocks of lung and brain tissue from 1918 Spanish flu victims. The list shows the names of some children who died from the flu during the 1918 pandemic.

pandemic because no one has developed antibodies against it. Without previous antibodies to defend against it, a new flu strain spreads with frightening speed and continues to infect new hosts wherever it travels.

In 1918, an influenza pandemic began that was so devastating it killed between 20 and 50 million people worldwide in the span of little more than a year. More than a half-million people died in the United states alone. Between 20 and 40 percent of the world's population was affected by the pandemic before it was over. Imagine what it would be like if nearly half of the people in your family, your neighborhood, your school, and your town came down with the same deadly illness at the same time. Millions of people experienced such losses during the flu pandemic of 1918.

The virus that caused the pandemic starting in 1918 did not behave like a typical flu virus. Unlike the majority of flu viruses, which kill mostly elderly people, the 1918 version killed millions of young, healthy adults, sometimes within days and even within hours. Some flu experts now believe that people over 65 may have had effective antibodies from previous flu epidemic that struck in the mid-1800s. Younger people who had not been born during that earlier epidemic were completely unprotected against the 1918 flu.

The pandemic of 1918 is often referred to as the Spanish flu because the deadly illness was first recognized as a flu pandemic in Spain. But it left a trail of destruction around the

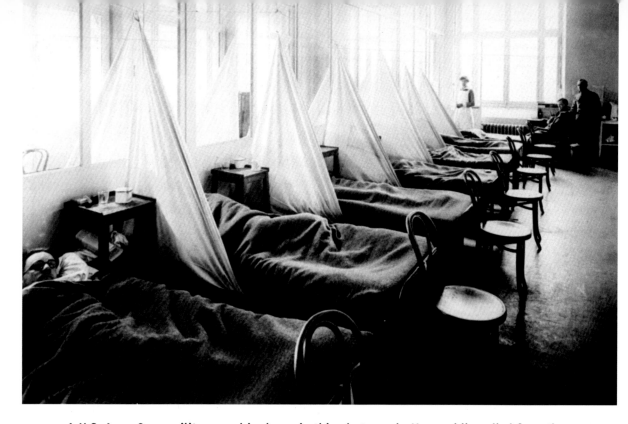

A U.S. Army Camp military ward is shown in this photograph. More soldiers died from the 1918 flu pandemic than were killed in battle during all of World War I.

world. The Spanish flu started in March 1918 and lasted through the spring of 1919. It is believed that the virus began in the United States and that some of the earliest cases of the pandemic sickened soldiers at an army base in Kansas. At first, people were not overly concerned about the outbreak since it did not affect the rest of the United States much at all. It is possible that many people had partial antibodies—or immunity—and that these antibodies were able to stop the virus from spreading very far after the initial infection.

During the spring and summer of 1918, United States troops joined the fighting in Europe during World War I. Along with their guns and supplies, the troops may have also carried with them the deadliest flu virus in history. The flu spread wherever the soldiers went, then was passed on to the French, British, Italian, and Spanish soldiers by the end of May 1918. The flu traveled beyond Europe and quickly infected North Africa, China, India, and Japan, all before the end of spring. It continued to spread, and Russia, New Zealand, the Caribbean and Central America were all affected.

By the end of the summer of 1918, people in all these countries died in record numbers in just a few months' time. Just when the worst seemed to be over, however, the virus reappeared. On its second reappearance in the United States, the virus was stronger than before. Scientists believe that the virus mutated after the spring and summer into an even deadlier form. Many people lacked antibodies to this changed form and faced it without any protection. Throughout the fall and winter of 1918, large numbers of people continued to become infected and die.

Victor Vaughan was a doctor during the Spanish flu pandemic. In September 1918, he went to Camp Devens outside of Boston, Massachusetts, to help treat the sick and dying soldiers. On the day Dr. Vaughan arrived at the military camp, 63 men died of influenza. Dr. Vaughan described what he saw at Camp Devens and called it the saddest part of his life. He could do nothing to help the hundreds of young men

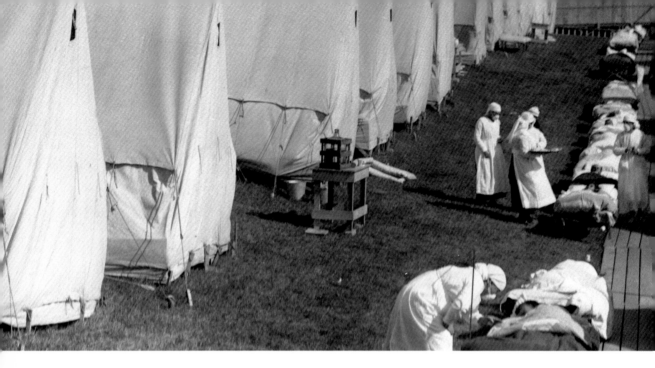

Health officials during the 1918 pandemic sent some patients to be treated at fresh-air camps like this one in Maine.

who died. "I saw hundreds of young stalwart [strong] men in uniform coming into the wards of the hospital," Dr. Vaughan wrote. "Every bed was full, yet others crowded in. The faces wore a bluish cast [appearance]; a cough brought up the blood-stained sputum [mucus]." Dr. Vaughan studied what influenza was doing to the soldiers and tried his best to help them. He was among the first to realize that this flu was unlike any other flu people had experienced.

Even after World War I was over, in November 1918, the war against influenza continued to rage. The disease continued its destructive attack through the winter and into the spring of 1919. The flu pandemic finally collapsed when it eventually ran out of potential hosts and lost momentum.

By the time it was over, the pandemic had caused more damage than World War I. It had killed many millions and disrupted the social and economic systems of dozens of countries. Finally, by May 1919, the Spanish flu pandemic was over.

While the Spanish flu may have been the deadliest influenza pandemic in recorded history, it is not the only one. In 1957, the Asian flu pandemic killed more than one million people worldwide and approximately 70,000 in the United States alone. This pandemic killed mostly elderly people and lasted about one year. The virus had begun in China and traveled to the United

The Asian flu outbreak of 1957 emptied out offices and classrooms. This teacher normally had thirty students in her class.

States, where scientists quickly identified it and created a vaccine against it. Interestingly, this Asian flu virus contained a combination of human and **avian** (relating to birds) influenza genes. This means that the virus mutated in such a way that some humans caught the flu from birds. From then on, humans with that form of avian virus infected each other.

Another pandemic involved the Hong Kong flu, named after the place it was first detected in early 1968. This virus killed roughly 34,000 people in the United States and more than one million people globally. Like the Asian flu, the Hong Kong flu virus was a combination of human and avian influenza genes that affected the elderly most seriously.

Learning from the past devastation, 40 million Americans were vaccinated in 1976 during the Swine flu scare. This flu had first sickened pigs and then infected humans. Luckily, the 1976 outbreak did not spread and turn into a pandemic.

Deadly flu epidemics or pandemics may occur when two or more flu viruses infect the same animal. Scientists have a theory that this deadly mix may happen in pigs. Pigs are the only mammals that are domesticated in large numbers and can serve as hosts for both avian and human influenza viruses. The close contact between humans and pigs could spread a new, remixed virus from pigs to humans that could lead to a catastrophic pandemic.

Two recent scares in 1997 and 1999 involved avian flu viruses previously thought to infect only birds. In the 1997

Computer model of bird flu strain H5N1. This deadly flu strain began infecting and killing some humans who had close contact with birds in Hong Kong in 1997.

avian flu scare, six people died in Hong Kong after becoming infected from local chickens. No new human infections were seen after all the chickens in Hong Kong were killed to prevent the spread of the virus.

Avian flu viruses may pose a serious threat to human health in the near future. Influenza viruses occur naturally among wild birds throughout the world and may have originated in wild ducks and shore birds that live near water. The virus does not always harm these wild birds, which act more like carriers than victims of the virus. Scientists discovered that wild aquatic, or water birds, carry a collection of all known influenza A virus subtypes without always getting sick from them. Infected wild birds spread the virus through their saliva, nasal secretions, and waste products. Avian flu viruses are very contagious among domesticated birds such as chickens, ducks, and turkeys. The birds can become very sick and even die. By early 2006, dozens of people in Asia and in Turkey who worked with, played with, or ate sick birds died of avian flu. Avian influenza A viruses may mutate slowly or suddenly, and then spread directly from human to human.

WORLDWIDE PREPARATIONS FOR THE FLU

Pandemic viruses are fairly rare and unpredictable. It is difficult to predict what conditions may cause a pandemic influenza virus to emerge. Preparation is the key to the successful avoidance of another pandemic. The United States has drafted a National Influenza Preparedness Plan. The World Health Organization has designed a global plan to handle an influenza health crisis equal to, or worse than, the 1918 Spanish flu pandemic.

Rapid communication among countries worldwide is key to coping with another pandemic like the one in 1918. Keeping

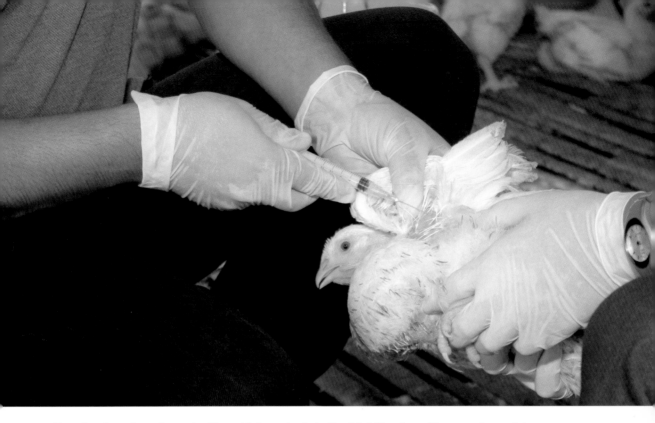

Veterinarians have been testing chickens in Asia for bird flu virus. They send suspicious samples to worldwide health organizations for further study in making a vaccine.

track of the influenza viruses through worldwide surveillance is an important part of keeping the world safe. There is another important part of pandemic preparedness planning: defining the roles and responsibilities of national and local governments and individuals in the community. This means that everyone needs to work together in an organized manner. Also, efforts to prevent contact between wild and domestic birds have successfully prevented outbreaks of influenza from spreading too far in domestic birds. In the recent outbreaks of avian flu that killed many birds, farmers and poultry sellers took drastic measures. They killed millions of their own birds to prevent the virus from mutating and spreading too far.

4

PREVENTING, DIAGNOSING, AND TREATING THE FLU

Personal contact is part of everyday life, even during the flu season. We usually talk with people every day at school or work, sit near them on buses and planes, and shop next to them in stores. We cannot help but pass through places where many people have also walked and possibly sneezed. Since people with the flu are infectious for a few days before they feel sick, it is nearly impossible to completely avoid contact with potentially sick people. Still, there are several important ways to help prevent catching the flu.

If you get the flu, drink plenty of liquids to prevent dehydration.

Avoid sharing food, eating utensils, or drinks with other people. Drinking from the same container, such as a glass or a sports bottle, is a quick way to share saliva that might carry the flu virus. Washing your hands is also a very important way to help stay healthy. The flu virus is often spread when you touch something contaminated, or the virus lands on you, and you touch your face. So try to avoid rubbing your eyes or touching your nose or mouth. Viruses waiting on doorknobs, staircase railings, telephones, or elevator buttons will not be able to make you sick if you wash them off your hands before they reach your nose or mouth.

Follow good habits all year long, but especially during flu season. Eat well-balanced

Flu Prevention

A simple and easy way to keep healthy is to keep washing your hands.

HOW?

- Wash with soap and warm water for half a minute.
- If there is no sink nearby, use alcohol-based wipes or hand gels to clean your hands.

WHEN:

- After using the bathroom.
- Before eating or handling food.
- After sneezing, coughing, or blowing your nose.
- After a trip to a public place, such as school, the library, grocery store, shopping mall, subway, bus, train, or plane.

meals and stay physically active. Eating whole grains, fruits, vegetables, and protein will help keep your immune system strong. Exercise has many benefits for your body. Staying fit strengthens your heart and lungs and increases your overall health. Smokers should stop smoking for their own health and for the health of people who live with them. Cigarette smoke irritates the lining of a smoker's nose and lungs, and the connective passages between them, which can increase the risk of flu-related **complications.** Nonsmokers who live with smokers suffer from some of these problems as well.

FLU SHOTS

While washing your hands, eating healthy, and staying physically fit can help prevent the flu, many believe that the best prevention is getting vaccinated if your doctor recommends it. **Immunization** against the flu is the process of protecting someone from the disease by giving him or her a highly weakened form of the flu virus in an injection. Your immune system recognizes invaders it has seen before, and vaccines like those for measles, polio, and influenza take advantage of this ability. A vaccine introduces a weakened, safe form of an invader into the body. This triggers antibody production in the immune system. If the real invader—like the flu virus—attacks later on, the immune system is ready and launches effective antibodies against the virus.

Vaccinations can protect you from the flu if you are exposed to the same influenza virus that matches the vaccine. Even when the vaccine does not totally prevent infection, it can help reduce the severity of symptoms and the risk of developing complications.

A flu vaccine contains a weakened form of flu viruses that scientists believe will infect people in a particular year.

Two different types of influenza vaccines are currently available. The first type contains viruses that have been killed, or **inactivated,** to trigger the immune system. This type is approved for use in everyone older than six months. People who have had a severe reaction to a flu shot in the past or are allergic to chicken eggs should not get a flu shot. The connection between flu shots and chicken eggs has to do with the way the vaccine is produced. Also, people who are allergic to a chemical called thimerosal should not get a flu shot because this chemical is usually part of the vaccine. If you are currently sick and have a fever, you should not get a flu shot while you are sick. But you can be vaccinated after you recover if your doctor advises this.

A second type of vaccine uses viruses that are still alive but weak enough so that they cannot cause a full infection. This vaccine is sprayed into the nose where it enters the cells lining the nose and nasal passages. It was approved by the United States Food and Drug Administration in 2003, but it cannot be used in certain groups of people. There is a greater chance of a person becoming sick from the vaccination itself because it contains components of live viruses. Therefore, people with ongoing health problems, pregnant women, children younger than five years old, and the elderly should not receive this type of vaccine. People with weak immune systems also should not receive this type of vaccine. They should even avoid contact with people who have been vaccinated this way for the first week after immunization. But such vulnerable populations should try to avoid sick people in general to avoid potential infection.

Whether live or man-made, the two types of influenza vaccines have both differences and similarities. The killed virus vaccine is injected with a needle, usually into the arm. It then enters the bloodstream and triggers antibody production. From this point on, both live and man-made vaccines work the same way. They cause the immune system to fight the infection with B-cells that create antibodies against the virus. The body produces antibodies that stick to the surface proteins of the virus.

Side effects from being vaccinated against the flu are usually mild and do not last more than one or two days. A mild fever, muscle aches, and redness or soreness around the injection site are potential side effects from the flu shot. The nasal vaccine may cause a low fever, runny nose, sore throat,

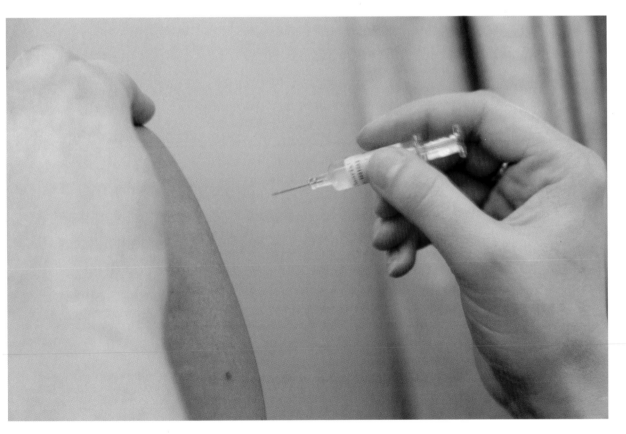

An injected vaccine stimulates the immune system to produce antibodies against the next possible flu infection.

or headache for the first few days. The few risks associated with the flu vaccine are small compared with the major benefits of helping to prevent severe outbreaks of influenza.

Most vaccines, like those for diseases such as hepatitis B and diptheria, last a lifetime. The influenza vaccine is different. A new one must be given every year to be effective. This is because influenza viruses change from year to year. Their protective benefit weakens over time. The antibodies your body produces after you get a vaccine may not be the right kind to fight the next type of influenza virus.

Vaccination does not immediately protect people from getting sick. It takes about two weeks after receiving the flu shot or nasal spray vaccine for your immune system to develop enough antibodies to prevent infection. People are still at risk of getting sick during that two-week period. That is why the best time to get immunized is in October or November, before the peak of flu season. How well the vaccine works depends on many factors, including the age and general health condition of the person receiving the vaccine. Success also depends on how closely the virus strains in the vaccine match the strains that are making people sick.

Both types of influenza vaccines actually contain three different virus strains—two type A strains and one type B. Each year, many laboratories all around the world collect flu viruses from sick patients. They send some of those virus samples to the World Health Organization to be tested. The World Health

Organization has four reference laboratories that do this special testing. One is in the United States at the Centers for Disease Control in Atlanta, Georgia. The labs test many of the viruses' features and then compare them to other current and past viruses. They also test the way antibodies against the current version of the flu vaccine react to the sample viruses.

Scientists developed the method for preparing flu vaccines inside fertilized chicken eggs more than fifty years ago.

How a Flu Vaccine Is Made

....

It takes several months to plan out and produce flu vaccines. Scientists are working on new ways to quickly produce large quantities of flu vaccine. But until a better process is discovered, most laboratories use the same process to manufacture flu vaccines.

First, in February and early March each year, several vaccine makers around the world receive millions of chicken eggs, which they sort into three batches. Each batch has one of the three flu strains injected into the fluid surrounding the embryo, or yolk, of each egg. The eggs are sealed shut. Over the course of several days, the virus strains copy themselves inside the eggs.

Laboratory workers break the eggs, collect the virus-filled fluid and the embryos, and purify this material. A chemical called formaldehyde is added to the material to inactivate the virus. This will ensure that the virus stops copying itself and will not copy itself once the vaccine is injected into people. (In the nasal-spray form of the vaccine, the virus is not killed. A very weakened form of the live virus is used.)

A machine separates out the material containing the virus. This separated virus material is injected into new eggs. Technicians wait to see if the virus is inactive and does not copy itself in these new eggs. If it is inactive, it can be used in a vaccine.

Laboratory technicians again purify the material of all the eggs. They then retest the material to make sure no germs are present that would contaminate—or dirty—the vaccine. The three viral strains are combined into the vaccine that will be given to people in the fall months that year.

A technician checks bottles of flu vaccine on an assembly line.

Doctors and scientific researchers present information about flu activity and the viruses to scientists. These scientists then predict which strains will be the most widespread and common. They use three of them to create that year's vaccine. Usually, one or two of the three virus strains are changed from year to year.

Once the strains are chosen for the vaccines, it takes several months to produce enough vaccine to send out to doctors around the world. Decisions on which viruses to include are made six to nine months in advance of actually making the vaccine and giving it to people. This advance decision-making means that scientists have to make their best guesses about which strains will be most likely to make people sick.

DIAGNOSIS

Despite healthy habits and flu shots, many people do get the flu during some outbreaks. So how do doctors know whether someone has the flu? They usually diagnose the flu based on symptoms alone: sudden onset of fever, aching muscles, coughing, runny nose, and watery, itchy eyes. Infectious disease experts, as well as local doctors, also monitor outbreaks of flu around the world and in their own communities. If many people have recently become infected with the flu, doctors are on the alert that an outbreak is underway. Therefore, most patients will not need any specific tests to confirm that they have the flu. However, doctors may recommend testing people who are most at risk for developing serious flu complications.

Exams and Tests

One kind of test allows researchers to analyze blood samples to see what antibodies are present. This flu test is not used often. Results can take up to two weeks, and by then the flu infection is usually over.

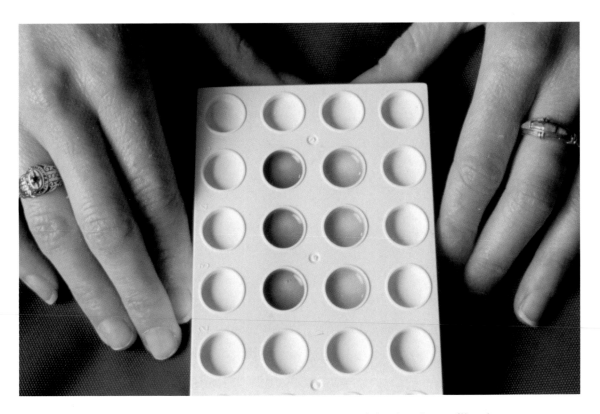

In one kind of influenza virus test, a nasal or throat swab is placed over film that covers these "wells." A color change in the film indicates flu virus is present in the swab sample.

In another test, researchers look for the influenza virus itself in mucus or fluid samples from the inside of a patient's nose or throat. Doctors have the swabbed samples checked for the presence of influenza virus. This method is faster—it takes three days to a week for results.

If doctors need results more quickly than that, other tests work even faster. Scientists have developed test kits that can detect the influenza virus within 24 hours. Other tests can deliver results within 30 minutes. However, they have limitations and might not be very accurate.

Despite the drawbacks of all current flu tests, doctors do order these tests for at-risk patients who seem likely to develop serious complications. Flu tests can help doctors plan treatments for such patients in advance.

COMPLICATIONS

Complications of the flu can develop in anyone. But a healthy person with a strong immune system will not usually develop serious problems. However, several populations are at risk for complications. These include very young children, people older than 65 years, and people with weakened immune systems. People who suffer from existing or continual medical problems like cancer, diabetes, and heart or lung disease are at risk for complications. Many of these same vulnerable people come into close contact in nursing homes, hospitals, and day care centers.

Complications may appear just when the flu infection seems to be over. Pneumonia, bronchitis, **dehydration,** and a worsening of pre-existing illnesses are all possible complications. Symptoms of these secondary illnesses are yellow or greenish discharge from the nose or throat, severe and constant coughing, reappearance of a fever, and greater exhaustion.

Pneumonia, a lung infection that can slow a person's breathing or shut it down, is one serious flu complication. Bronchitis is an **inflammation** of the bronchial breathing tubes that causes severe coughing. Both conditions can develop during the time someone has the flu. A person already sick with the flu who develops an infection from pneumonia or bronchitis is in a life-threatening condition and should seek medical attention immediately.

Dehydration is another potential problem. People sick with

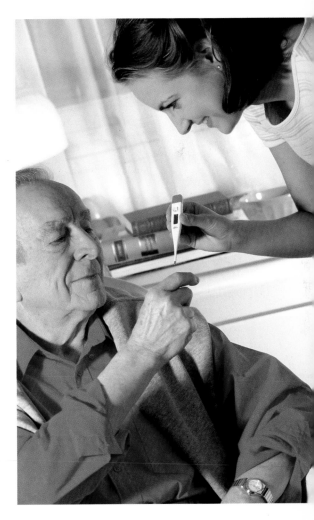

Health-care professionals carefully watch for flu complications in elderly patients.

Flu Treatment

DO NOT

- Push yourself too hard to return to normal activities.
- Take aspirin.
- Take a cold bath to reduce fever.
- Share drinks or food with anyone when you are sick.
- Sneeze or cough without covering your nose and mouth.

DO

- Get plenty of rest.
- Drink water, juice, or other fluids to keep hydrated.
- Take a nonaspirin pain reliever to reduce fever and muscle aches.
- See a health-care professional if any symptoms become severe, or if you experience difficulty breathing, fast breathing, or chest pains.

the flu usually develop high fevers and sweat a lot. They also lose bodily fluids through coughing and sneezing. These fluids need to be replaced. If a sick person does not drink enough fluids, he or she may become dehydrated. Severe dehydration damages the cells in major organs like the brain, kidneys, lungs, heart, and liver, which need water to keep them working properly. Quick medical attention is needed to replace bodily fluids before such damage takes place.

For people who already have other health problems, a case of the flu can sometimes worsen those illnesses. This is especially true of people who have heart or lung diseases, asthma, or diabetes. In very young children, ear infections and sinus problems are common complications. The sinuses are air-filled spaces in the head behind the forehead, cheeks, and eyes that are lined with membranes. Healthy sinuses are wide open and do not contain bacteria. When problems arise due to the flu, sinuses can become infected. This complication may require separate medical attention.

Treatment

Home treatment is usually all that is needed to recover from a typical case of the flu. Symptoms usually go away in five to seven days when people stay home, get plenty of rest, drink fluids, and take a nonaspirin pain reliever such as ibuprofen or

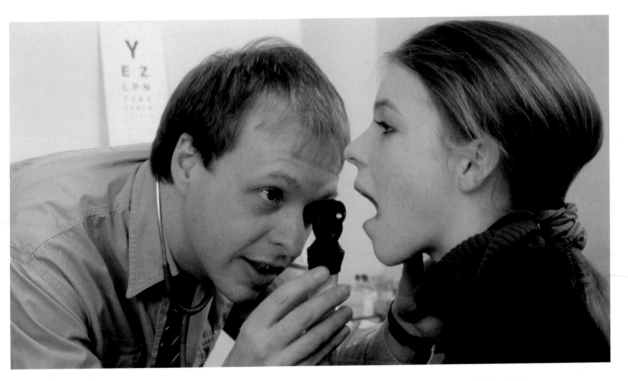

Anyone suffering from any severe flu symptoms that last more than a week should be seen by a doctor.

Resting at home is the most effective way to recover from the flu and keep the virus from spreading to others.

acetaminophen. Aspirin should not be used to treat fever or muscle aches associated with the flu, or any other viral infection. Doing so increases the risk of developing a condition called Reye's syndrome, which can cause liver failure and swelling in the brain.

One of the most important treatments for the flu is getting plenty of rest. Fatigue may last longer than any other symptom, so sleep and general inactivity will help you charge up your energy. A health-care professional may advise decongestants or a nasal spray to unclog a stuffy nose. Drinking plenty of fluids may help provide relief from coughing, and prevent dehydration.

When a person has a fever, the goal should be to lower

it, but not completely, so that this natural infection-fighting mechanism is not taken away. Fever often makes people alternate between feeling excessively hot and then very cold. If the person has the chills, he or she should not be too bundled up. Use layers and keep the person warm but not smothered. Remove excess clothing or heavy blankets. A lukewarm bath may help cool the person down, but never use very cold water. That could cause shivering, which actually raises the body's internal temperature instead of lowering it. Drinking cool liquids and circulating air with a fan may also help take the heat out of having a fever.

While most people recover completely through home care methods, people experiencing certain symptoms should seek medical attention instead of treating themselves at home. Some of these warning signs are difficulty breathing, fast breathing, and chest pains. These can be signs of more serious problems such as asthma, pneumonia, or heart disease. Doctors may test for a secondary infection or internal injury if a person has a long-lasting fever, congestion, or serious pain when swallowing. A person who experiences dizziness, confusion, or has difficulty waking up, needs urgent medical attention. Excessive vomiting may lead to dehydration and requires medical treatment. Also, if a person's skin appears bluish, he or she may not be getting enough oxygen and should see a doctor immediately.

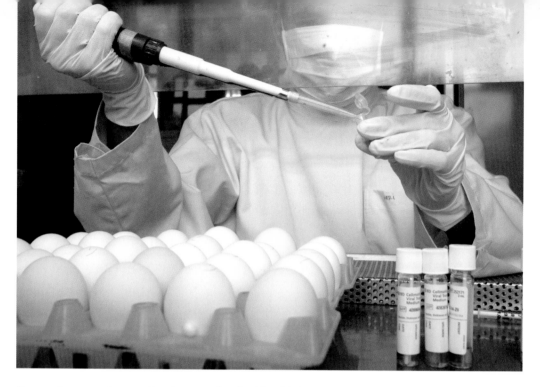

Researchers must grow flu virus strains inside chicken eggs, a time-consuming process that does not always result in an effective flu vaccine.

THE FUTURE OF THE FLU

The current method of traditional vaccine production is time-consuming. To select and grow the seed strains, researchers must have 270 million chicken eggs on hand in which to plant the seed strains. Then they must wait for the viruses to grow, a step that takes many months from start to finish. If scientists' predictions about which strains will be most common are wrong, there is little that can be done that year to change the vaccine. It probably will not be effective. Starting over is nearly impossible. It requires too much time, work, and material to remake the vaccine.

That is why researchers are trying to invent new and better

ways to create vaccines. One new way uses genetic material from cells to create strains that match the current influenza virus exactly. Then the scientists grow this material in large tanks instead of using chicken eggs. This technique, called **cell culture,** requires less time and work. Vaccines produced this way may turn out to be a good option for people who are allergic to chicken eggs. It is also much easier and faster to grow cells this way. They can be frozen in advance and then thawed and grown quickly when needed. As in all areas of medicine and science, technology will continue to improve the way influenza vaccines are produced.

Vaccine Supplies

A vaccine shortage in 2004 highlighted some of the problems with flu vaccine production, as well as more general issues involved in preparing for a major influenza epidemic or pandemic. Some of the viral strains circulating today are already **resistant** to certain available antiviral drugs and are not killed or slowed down by that drug. Resistance is one trait that can be developed through mutation, and it can be either a gradual or rapid change. Preventing another influenza pandemic will depend on current and future preparation, research, and resources dedicated to investigating and understanding the flu.

Recent studies have shown that a flu vaccination can be 70 to 90 percent effective at preventing infection. But this is when the viruses chosen for a year's vaccine match the viruses that are actually in circulation that year. That is a major reason why a faster method of vaccine production is needed. If we could wait to produce vaccines until the most common viruses are known for sure, and not go on scientists' best guesses months in advance, influenza vaccines would be more effective against the circulating viruses.

If scientists continue to improve the way flu vaccines are made, fewer people will have to suffer through the flu each year. Researchers will still have to monitor the flu viruses and track mutations in order to update the vaccines. A vaccine against the avian flu viruses may eventually be created. This could help limit the possibility that the current avian flu strain will cause the next influenza pandemic. Viruses will keep changing, and we will have to keep changing our technology to keep up with them.

GLOSSARY

antibodies—The proteins produced by cells in response to a foreign substance.

antigens—The substances present on a pathogen that allow the immune system to recognize the pathogen as foreign.

avian—Relating to birds.

bone marrow—The soft tissue inside bones, which contains many blood vessels and produces red and white blood cells.

cell culture—A technique for growing cells in a laboratory.

clot—The formation of a mass of cells and proteins to stop bleeding.

complications—Diseases or conditions that develop during the course of or as a result of another disease or illness.

contagious—Easily passed on by contact between individuals.

dehydration—The excessive loss of water and body fluids.

epidemic—A sudden, rapid outbreak of disease that spreads widely and affects many individuals at one time.

genes—The parts of cells containing information that determines an individual's traits.

hosts—The humans, animals, or plants that a parasite such as a fungus or virus lives in or on.

immune system—The system that protects the body from foreign substances, cells, and infection by recognizing these foreign invaders and destroying them.

immunization—A treatment with a vaccine to prevent the development of a specific disease.

inactivate—To destroy certain biological activities of a virus in order to make it unable to infect and cause harm.

infectious—Able to spread infection.

inflammation—The swelling of tissues due to an infection or injury.

leukocytes—All white blood cells.

lymphatic system—A system of special tissues, including the lymph nodes, that filters and destroys foreign material.

lymph nodes—The structures found throughout the immune system where white blood cells form and lymph fluid is filtered.

lymphocytes—The white blood cells that are either B-cells or T-cells.

microbe—A microorganism or germ.

microorganisms—Tiny organisms of microscopic or less than microscopic size.

molecules—Small units of an organism or object involved in chemical reactions.

mutates—To change the genetic material of an organism.

pandemic—The widespread infection by one type of virus that affects many people in different parts of the world at nearly the same time.

parasites—Organisms that live in or on other living things, called hosts.

pathogens—Bacteria or viruses that can cause disease.

phagocytes—The large white blood cells that can destroy microbes, other cells, and foreign particles by engulfing them.

proteins—The complex substances in cells that are necessary to carry out essential life functions.

resistant—Unaffected by treatment with a certain drug.

respiratory—Related to breathing processes.

strains—The related groups of influenza viruses that have slightly different characteristics.

symptoms—Physical conditions that indicate the presence of a disease or other disorder.

vaccine—A preparation of killed, weakened, or fully infectious microbes that is given (often by injection) to provide protection from a particular disease.

virus—A particle able to multiply and cause disease within an organism.

FIND OUT MORE

Books

Isle, Mick. *Everything You Need to Know About Colds and Flu.* New York: The Rosen Group, 2004.

Peters, Stephanie True. *Epidemic! The 1918 Influenza Pandemic.* New York: Benchmark Books, 2005.

Stedman, Nancy. *Understanding Disease: The Common Cold and Influenza.* New York: Simon and Schuster, 1989.

Web Sites

BAM! Body and Mind—Centers for Disease Control and Prevention (CDC)
http://www.bam.gov

KidsHealth for Kids: The Flu
http://www.kidshealth.org/kid/ill_injure/flu/flu.html

National Institute of Allergies and Infectious Diseases (NIAID): Focus on the Flu
http://www3.niaid.nih.gov/news/focuson/flu/default.htm

World Health Organization: Influenza
http://www.who.int/topics/influenza/en/

INDEX

Page numbers for illustrations are in **boldface**

ABOUT THE AUTHOR

Gretchen Hoffmann has always been fascinated by science and enjoys learning and writing about science and health. Her special interest in infectious diseases led her to do research in a lab studying viruses after graduating from Cornell University. In addition to *The Flu,* Ms. Hoffmann is the author of another Health Alert title, *Mononucleosis,* and has also published in Scholastic's classroom magazine, *Science World.* Currently she works as a medical writer at a medical communication company and lives with her husband, Bill, in Valhalla, New York.